THE
SHAWNEE INDIANS

THE JUNIOR LIBRARY OF AMERICAN INDIANS

THE SHAWNEE INDIANS

Terrance Dolan

CHELSEA JUNIORS

ON THE COVER: Detail from a painting by Seth Eastman of an Indian sugar camp, courtesy W. Duncan MacMillan.

FRONTISPIECE: Straight Man, a Shawnee painted in 1830 by George Catlin.

CHAPTER TITLE ORNAMENT: A Shawnee beadwork design.

English-language words that are italicized in the text can be found in the glossary at the back of the book.

Chelsea House Publishers
EDITORIAL DIRECTOR Richard Rennert
EXECUTIVE MANAGING EDITOR Karyn Gullen Browne
COPY CHIEF Robin James
PICTURE EDITOR Adrian G. Allen
CREATIVE DIRECTOR Robert Mitchell
ART DIRECTOR Joan Ferrigno
PRODUCTION MANAGER Sallye Scott

The Junior Library of American Indians
SENIOR EDITOR Martin Schwabacher

Staff for THE SHAWNEE INDIANS
ASSISTANT EDITOR Catherine Iannone
EDITORIAL ASSISTANT Erin McKenna
DESIGNER Lydia Rivera
PICTURE RESEARCHER Sandy Jones

3 5 7 9 8 6 4 2

Library of Congress Cataloging-in-Publication Data

Dolan, Terrance
The Shawnee Indians/ Terrance Dolan
  p. cm. — (The Junior Library of American Indians)
Includes index.
      0-7910-1673-0
      0-7910-2035-5 (pbk.)
1. Shawnee Indians—History—Juvenile literature. 2. Shawnee
Indians—Social life and customs—Juvenile literature. [1. Shawnee
Indians. 2. Indians of North America.] I. Title. II. Series.
E99.S35D65 1996   95-11972
973'.04973—dc20   CIP
                                                   AC

CONTENTS

CHAPTER 1

The Breaking of the Belt

In early March 1779, at the Shawnee town of Chalahgawtha, the Shawnees gathered within the huge *msi-kah-mi-qui*—the high-roofed council house. Assembled there were all the male principal chiefs, warriors, and spiritual leaders of the Shawnee nation. Also present were the tribal mothers—respected female warriors and healers and other women who had displayed wisdom and leadership.

Each of the five divisions of the Shawnee nation had sent representatives to the council fire. The five divisions were the Mekoches, Chalahgawthas, Pekowis, Thawikilas, and Kishpokos. Chalahgawtha might be con-

This painting of a Shawnee chief named Goes Up the River shows the style of dress at the time of the council at Chalahgawtha. Many Shawnee men slit and stretched their earlobes to form long loops.

7

sidered the capital town of the Shawnee nation during this period. (The town where the principal chief of the five Shawnee divisions lived was often named after that chief's tribe or after the chief himself.) Chalahgawtha was located along the Little Miami River in Ohio. The town's packed-earth avenues and side streets were lined with over 1,000 *wegiwas* —houses built of wood poles and broad strips of bark.

By March 9, hundreds of tipis had been set up around the outskirts of the town as the visitors arrived for the council. Many visitors were invited to stay in the wegiwas of friends and relatives. In the center of Chalahgawtha was the town's msi-kah-mi-qui. A rectangular wooden structure, this msi-kah-mi-qui was fully 120 feet long and 40 feet wide. The large main entrance was covered with buffalo hides. Within, five columns supported the 20-foot-high roof.

The representatives of the five Shawnee divisions waited in the msi-kah-mi-qui. They were seated on the floor in circles around the council fire, which burned slowly in the center of the council house. The smallest circle, closest to the fire, was reserved for the highest ranking chiefs. In a larger circle around these principal chiefs sat those of slightly lesser rank and honor. And so, in ever widening circles, the msi-kah-mi-qui was filled to its wooden walls.

Everyone was dressed for the occasion in the finest ceremonial manner. The men wore traditional Shawnee clothing—deerskin pants, some fringed and some with a stripe painted down the side; deerskin shirts; and breechcloths. Many also wore clothing obtained through trade or battle with white men. The long brass-buttoned overcoats of white military officers were especially favored. The men decorated their bodies with silver wristlets and armbands, heavy silver hoop earrings, small nose rings, otter-skin turbans, and the traditional single-feathered headdress fastened to a knot of hair at the back of the head. Moccasins skillfully embroidered with colored beads and dyed porcupine quills were a part of each man's dress. Deerskin or elk-skin shoulder bags and heavy blankets, folded up and worn like a sash over one shoulder and around the upper body, were carried by almost all of the men. Tucked into their belts were their most finely decorated tomahawks, which also served as long-stemmed smoking pipes. The handle was hollowed out and the bowl for smoking was on the opposite side of the blade. Knives, war clubs, and an occasional Euro-

pean sword or pistol were also carried. Bows and arrows and rifles had been left behind in the tents and wegiwas. The men painted their faces with a straight red line or a series of three lines—like rays of red sunlight—drawn outward from the corners of their eyes. Those who wore three lines might place a red dot between each line.

The Shawnee women were dressed in simple deerskin skirts, leggings, and moccasins. Some women wore leggings with tiny round bells sewn into them, which tinkled musically when they walked. Some wore white cotton blouses. The womens' long,

In 1750, British explorers discovered the Cumberland Gap, a low pass through the Cumberland Mountains of Virginia, Kentucky, and Tennessee. This discovery made it easy for white settlers to drive their wagons into Shawnee territory.

glossy black hair was parted in the middle and was not covered by any headdress, although some of them fastened their hair in a bun with a silver comb. Many of the women also wore bead necklaces and silver bracelets. Most did not decorate their face, although some might place a small red dot on one or both cheeks.

Within the council house, the atmosphere was dim and smoky—and grim. Here and there could be heard a tense, whispered exchange of words. Silence fell with the smoking of the calumets—the ceremonial council pipes. Three feet long, fashioned from hickory, and painted with colorful images of animals and other symbolic designs, the two pipes were brought in already lighted and presented to the principal chief of the Shawnee nation—Chiungalla of the Chalahgawthas. The principal chief smoked from each pipe, then passed one to the principal war chief and one to the principal peace chief, who were seated behind and to either side of Chiungalla. They smoked and passed the pipes on. When all had smoked, the council began.

Everyone present knew the reason for the lighting of the council fire at Chalahgawtha— the *Shemanese* (the white men). The principal chief of the Thawikilas, elderly Kikusgowlowa, requested permission to speak first. This was uncommon. Usually the principal chief of the entire Shawnee nation spoke first. But Kikusgowlowa was highly respected and influential, and so Chiungalla graciously granted him permission.

Around the fire at the center of the council hall was an open space from which speakers addressed the assembly. Kikusgowlowa stood and slowly made his way to this spot. He rested a moment, leaning on a cane carved from a stout tree branch, and prepared to speak. What he said and did next shocked, angered, and dismayed the representatives of the Shawnee nation.

Looking around at the gathered Shawnees, the old chief began to speak. The Shawnees, Kikusgowlowa said, had battled the Shemanese for many years. Along with other tribes, they had filled the forests of the Kentucky hunting grounds with the corpses of the invaders. They had turned the waters of the Ohio River red with the invaders' blood. They had smashed the armies of the invaders in the Ohio and Kentucky territories and even as far east as Pennsylvania.

But for every dead Shemanese, ten, twenty, fifty more came to take his place. And for every defeated Shemanese army, an army three times the size followed;

armies that destroyed Shawnee villages, killed their livestock, and burned the corn in the fields, leaving the villagers to suffer through the harsh winter with little food, clothing, or shelter.

Even in victory, how many Shawnee warriors and chiefs had been killed during the years of war? How many captured? How many Shawnee wives had become

This shoulder bag from the early 19th century was decorated with colorful glass beads that were obtained from European traders.

widows, and children left fatherless? How many times had settlements been abandoned as the Shawnees were once again forced to move away from their enemies? The Shawnees could defeat the Shemanese in battle, but they could never drive them away permanently.

Old Kikusgowlowa was silent then. He leaned heavily on his cane and stared at the floor. Then he looked up again and continued. Now, he said, in the heart of Shawnee lands, Shemanese armies were building forts that were full of soldiers and defended by the thunder guns that killed many warriors with a single, booming shot. With the protection of the soldiers, the Shemanese settlers came boldly down the Ohio River and filled the forests and fields with their homes and ranches and livestock, as if these lands belonged to *them*. And, it seemed, these lands now did. For how could the Shawnees hope to defeat such an enemy—an enemy that returned again and again as surely as the harsh winter winds and snows?

The white allies of the Shawnees—the British—were clearly on the verge of defeat in the revolutionary war against those who called themselves the Americans. Soon, the Americans would turn their full attention on the

By the late 18th century, white settlers were taking over much of Shawnee territory. Boonesborough, shown here in 1778, was founded by the famous frontiersman Daniel Boone.

Shawnees and the other tribes that had fought alongside the British. To continue fighting the Shemanese would mean the destruction of the Shawnees. They would be swept away like dry leaves before the coming of the winds made by the beating of the Thunderbirds' wings. They would be broken to pieces and hurled to the sky like an old dead tree in the path of the Cyclone Person.

He had warned them all many times before, Kikusgowlowa reminded those gathered around him, that if the Shawnees continued to raise the tomahawk against the

Americans, he would break the sacred bond that united the five Shawnee divisions; he would lead his people away and fight the Americans no more. Now, that time had come, for they were tired of shedding their blood and being driven like sheep before a power that was greater than their own.

Again, the old chief was silent. All the eyes surrounding him—the eyes of the Shawnee nation—watched as Kikusgowlowa reached

Native Americans often fell victim to the wars between whites. In 1782, Pennsylvania militiamen massacred 96 unarmed Delaware Indians because they wrongly suspected the Delawares of aiding the British.

into his shoulder bag and withdrew the sacred Shawnee Unity Belt. Five feet long and three inches wide, the belt had five sections. Each section was decorated with beads of a different color: blue, white, green, yellow, and red. Each color represented one of the five Shawnee divisions. The belt—as old as the Shawnee nation itself—represented the bond of unity that held the five divisions together as one people and one nation. Throughout Shawnee history, the sacred belt had been kept and protected by the Thawikilas.

Kikusgowlowa hung the belt from a peg in one of the wooden columns of the council house. He then produced from his blanket a tomahawk. Quickly, and with a terrible finality, he swung the tomahawk, chopping the belt in two pieces. Gasps and cries of anger, surprise, and even pain filled the council house. Three sections of the belt dropped to the floor—the sections representing the Thawikila, Pekowi, and Kishpoko divisions.

The elderly Kikusgowlowa stooped over with difficulty and picked up the three sections of the belt, holding them up for all to see. The brotherhood of the Shawnee nation was forever broken, he announced. The belt could never be reunited. He would lead the

Thawikilas, Pekowis, and Kishpokos away from their war-torn homeland, leaving forever the Mekoches and Chalahgawthas. The parting of the ways would be final.

The vast majority of the Thawikilas, Pekowis, and Kishpokos had already thrown their support behind Kikusgowlowa. Some of the warriors and lesser chiefs elected to stay behind with the Mekoches and Chalahgawthas, vowing never to lay down the tomahawk as long as the Shemanese continued to steal their lands.

Ten days after the council, Kikusgowlowa departed, followed by the representatives of the three breakaway divisions. They would be joined by the remainder of their people as they journeyed to the southwest, crossing the Mississippi River and settling for a time with the Creek peoples of Spanish Louisiana. They would find, however, that their *exodus* had only just begun.

For the two divisions who remained behind, determined to defend their homelands, the breakup could not have occurred at a worse time. More than two-thirds of their fighting force was now lost, just when they needed as many warriors as possible. At a time when not only their homelands but their *culture* itself—the essence of their way of life—was threatened, they had been unable to maintain the one thing that was most important in the face of such a crisis: unity.

The Shawnee nation would fight many battles during its long war with the invaders. It would win great victories and suffer crushing losses. But the most devastating defeat the Shawnees suffered occurred at their own hands, without a bullet fired by the Shemanese. This defeat occurred when Kikusgowlowa broke the sacred Unity Belt of the Shawnee nation.

CHAPTER 2

The Enigmatic Shawnees

Enigmatic is an appropriate description of the history and culture of the Shawnees. According to English dictionaries, the word *enigmatic* means "perplexing," "mysterious," "ambiguous," "riddle-like," and "difficult to define or to understand." The Shawnees were all of these and more.

As white settlers moved westward in search of new farmland, they cleared the woods in which Native Americans hunted and gathered food, and eventually they drove the Indians from their territory.

Europeans first came to North America in the late 15th century. Exploring the New World, as they called it, they discovered a huge continent stretching from ocean to ocean. North America was a place of remarkable beauty; a land of clear, sparkling rivers and streams, and lakes by the thousands. To the European explorers, it was a paradise rich in wildlife and natural resources; with environments that varied from parched desert to rainy, lush forest; from thousands of miles of flat plains to massive mountain ranges; from terrible heat to numbing cold.

The European newcomers also discovered that the "New World" was inhabited by peoples for whom North America was anything but new. From small tribes to great nations and alliances, the original Americans could be found in almost all of the various regions of the continent. Each of these peoples had *adapted* to their environment—whether it was the harsh desertlands of the Southwest or the dense forests of the Pacific coast. These peoples did more than adapt; they became one with their environment, as surely as the great timberwolf was one with the deep woodlands of the north and the buffalo was one with the Great Plains of Middle America.

During the centuries following the Europeans' arrival, their exploration of North America became a full-scale invasion. The European explorers eventually became American colonists and settlers who spread across the land from east to west like a great wave that never rolled back into the ocean from which it first came. The original peoples of North America were gradually but relentlessly driven from their homelands. Many of the smaller tribes simply vanished, washed away in the flood of invasion, the wars of resistance, and the epidemics of disease brought over from Europe. The histories of a large number of smaller tribes have been lost. Even their tribal names have been forgotten.

Because of their size, military strength, and the major role they played in the relations between white culture and Indian culture, the histories of the larger Indian tribes and nations are best known. For example, powerful or populous Indian groups such as the Ojibwas of the northern United States and Canada; the Iroquois Confederacy of the Northeast; the Sioux of the northern Great Plains; the Pueblo peoples of the Southwest; the Cherokees of the Southeast; and the Inuits of the Arctic are among the Indian tribes about which the most has been learned.

Compared to these peoples, little is known about the Shawnees. They remain, to this day, among the most enigmatic of the original American peoples. Yet the Shawnees were numerous and powerful. They played a crucial part in the interaction between the Indians of North America and the European

A French artist traveling through present-day Illinois produced this engraving of a Shawnee man in 1796.

newcomers, and in the bloody wars between the early United States and the Indians. Few tribes interacted with white people—both in peace and in war—more than the Shawnees. And no single tribe interacted with as many other Indian tribes as the Shawnees.

The Shawnees have had a strong relationship with white people from the time they encountered the first French and British fur traders and explorers. Intermarriage between Shawnees and European traders, and then

American settlers, was common. And a remarkable number of white people actually became Shawnees. These were children of white settlers who were captured and raised as Shawnees, and men and women who were captured and adopted into the tribe. Many of these men and women came to prefer the Shawnee way of life over their previous existence—so much so that when they were given a chance to return to white "civilization," they refused to leave their adopted community.

The Shawnee view of culture and humanity, unlike the view of most of the white Christian peoples who invaded their lands, was nonracist. Skin color had nothing to do with being a Shawnee. Accepting, understanding, and participating in the Shawnee way of life were what made a person a Shawnee, regardless of the person's previous existence or the color of his or her skin.

One of the greatest of all Shawnee leaders was a white man. He had been captured in 1771, at age 17, in a Shawnee raid on his parents' frontier settlement in western Virginia. He was wearing a blue hunting jacket when he was captured, so the Shawnees named him Blue Jacket. The Shawnee way of life appealed so much to Blue Jacket that he embraced it with his entire being. (Perhaps what appealed most to him was the opportunity to leave behind his original name: Marmaduke van Swearingen.)

Blue Jacket thrived as a Shawnee. He rose to become principal chief of the Mekoche division, and then second principal war chief of the entire Shawnee nation. Blue Jacket was a tireless and deadly foe of the whites who were driving the Shawnees and the other tribes from their lands, and he led Shawnee warriors in some of their greatest military triumphs over the forces of the She-manese. Although few achieved Blue Jacket's status within the tribe, many white men became Shawnee warriors and fought against the white invaders.

In Blue Jacket's time, white Americans were well aware of the Shawnees. The most remarkable figure to appear in late-18th- and early-19th-century North American history—either the history of the newcomers or the history of the original occupants—was a Shawnee named Tecumseh. But today, few non–Native Americans even recognize his name, although most have heard of such Indian leaders as Crazy Horse, Sitting Bull, and Geronimo.

Considering the Shawnees' important place in American history, it is hard to understand why their past remains such a mystery. Even the Shawnees are unsure of where they originated as a people. The region they eventually came to regard as their homeland—the Ohio River valley, mid- to northern Kentucky, western Pennsylvania, and southern Indiana—was not the region from which they originally came. The question of their origins is part of the mystery of the Shawnees.

Determining exactly where the Shawnees first lived is difficult for a number of reasons. The Shawnees did not record their own history in any form of writing or symbol drawing. Instead they had an *oral history* that was passed on from generation to generation, and there are many different versions of their history among the tribe. Also, as far back as their oral history reaches, the Shawnees were constantly on the move. Their story is, in many ways, the search for a homeland where they might permanently establish themselves. Yet their history is one of migration and scattering.

Often, the Shawnees were forced to move by hostile tribes such as the powerful Iroquois Confederacy and, later, by the Shemanese invaders and the U.S. government. But just as often, they moved voluntarily, breaking into small groups that traveled in opposite directions, settling for a period in a certain region, interacting—either peacefully or violently—with the tribes of that region, and then moving on once again. The Shawnees seem to have suffered from a kind of tribal restlessness.

The Shawnees traveled so widely and interacted with so many tribes that they inherited bits and pieces of numerous Indian cultures. This has proved confusing to anyone exploring the history and culture of the Shawnees, adding to their enigmatic character as a tribe. Some historians believe the Shawnees originated in an area known as the Fort Ancient region in southern Ohio, southern Indiana, northern Kentucky, and western West Virginia. But the oldest and most important aspects of Shawnee culture are shared with the tribes of the far northern woodlands. This suggests that in their most distant past the Shawnees lived among these peoples.

The Shawnees' traditional tribal history begins with the story of a journey: the crossing of what is described as a "lake," a "sea," or a "lake of ice." Although there are many versions of the tribe's origins and travels among the Shawnees, this one concept—the crossing of a body of water—remains constant, providing a clue to their original homeland. The "sea" or "lake" could

Shawnee traditions offer a clue to the tribe's origins. Many aspects of Shawnee culture, including religious beliefs and the type of homes they built, are also found among the Ojibwas of the northern Great Lakes region. Here, a shaman chants while preparing a mixture.

be one of the Great Lakes or a lake farther north in Canada, which the Shawnees crossed as they moved south.

Certain cultural similarities with tribes that lived in the lower Great Lakes region—in northern Michigan, Wisconsin, New York, and southern Canada—are prominent among the Shawnees. Other evidence indicates that the Shawnees originated in the upper Great Lakes region, perhaps as far north as the Lake Winnipeg area of Mani-

Lake Superior

CANADA

Huron

MICHIGAN

Lake Huron

ONTARIO

Lake Michigan

Lake Ontario

NEW

Potawatomi

Lake

Thames River

Detroit

Fort Malden→

Iroquois

YORK

Fort Miamis

Lake Erie

PENNSYLVANIA

•Cleveland

Tippecanoe River

Fort Meigs

Maumee River

Delaware

ProphʼtseTown

River

OHIO

•Fort Pitt
(Pittsburgh)

Wabash

Fort Greenville

Scioto River

Kickapoo

INDIANA

Ohio River

Fort Washington
(Cincinnati)

Miami

SHAWNEE

•Vincennes

Ohio River

WEST
VIRGINIA

KENTUCKY

0   150 miles

In 1725, the Shawnees settled north of the Ohio River, on land given to them by the Miamis.

toba, Canada. The Menominee tribe, who inhabited what is now upper Wisconsin and northern Michigan, assert that the Shawnees lived among them for a period in the distant past. Most striking, however, are similarities between the Shawnees and the mighty Ojibwa, or Chippewa, tribe.

At the height of their power, the Ojibwas' territory stretched throughout the Great Lakes region, including parts of present-day Michigan, Wisconsin, and Ontario, Canada, reaching as far east as Detroit and as far west as North Dakota. Among the many similarities between the Ojibwas and the Shawnees are the tradition of the sacred bundle, burial rites for the deceased, the use of animal names for family clans, and the form of housing used by both peoples.

A conflict with the powerful Ojibwas may have resulted in the Shawnees being driven from the region, much like the Sioux, the Fox, the Miamis, and numerous other tribes who were forced to remove themselves from the Ojibwa warpath. The possibility that the Shawnees were driven from their original territory would explain their constant search for a permanent homeland. They most likely migrated south from the Ojibwa-dominated area, crossing one of the Great Lakes or another large lake farther north. Like most of the northern woodlands tribes, the Shawnees were expert canoe builders and waterway navigators.

Moving down into the lower Great Lakes region in the mid-17th century, the Shawnees found themselves in the midst of chaotic warfare among the Iroquois Confederacy, the Huron tribe, and growing numbers of French, English, and Dutch traders, all of whom were competing for control of the region's fur trade. Finding themselves under repeated attack by the fearsome Iroquois Confederacy, the Shawnees broke into small groups and scattered. The various bands wandered in all directions. One band moved into the Ohio territory and the Susquehanna River valley of Pennsylvania. Another headed southeast into Georgia. Others traveled to Illinois. Some Shawnee bands settled in western Virginia, while others moved into the lower Lake Michigan region.

Throughout this period, the various Shawnee bands established themselves as warriors to be feared. When they were not under attack by a tribe whose hunting grounds they had wandered onto, they were joining other tribes, or the French or British, as allies in various wars and conflicts. The Shawnees often fought as mercenaries—soldiers for hire. René-Robert Cavalier de

continued on page 41

A SHAWNEE ARTIST

Despite the loss of their homeland and their relocation to reservations, the Shawnees have succeeded in retaining many of their traditions. The paintings of Shawnee artist Earnest Spybuck offer a glimpse at the Shawnees' way of life in the early 20th century. They reveal the ways in which the Shawnees held on to their ancient customs while adjusting to a constantly changing world.

Spybuck, an Absentee Shawnee of the Thawikila division, was born in Oklahoma in 1883. In 1910 his talent came to the attention of an anthropologist, who asked Spybuck to paint scenes of Native American life. These paintings provide valuable information about the ceremonies and the everyday life of the Shawnees and other tribes living on Oklahoma reservations.

Shawnee Indians Having Cornbread Dance (ca. 1910)

In Spybuck's time, the Bread Dance ceremony consisted of a three-day hunt by the men, followed by a feast prepared by the women. In this picture, the men have just returned from hunting and can be seen dancing in the background, while the women remove the resulting game from their horses.

Shawnee Home About 1890 (ca. 1910)

This painting recreates a scene from Spybuck's boyhood on the Absentee Shawnee Reservation in Oklahoma. Two hunters return with game while three women prepare food with a mix of traditional and manufactured utensils.

Sauk and Fox Drum Dance (ca. 1910)

by Earnest L. Spybuck

7644

Spybuck traveled to neighboring tribes to record their ceremonies as well as those of the Shawnees. This painting depicts a Sac and Fox religious ceremony called the Drum Dance or the Dream Dance. The white flags with red crosses on them are the symbol of a Sac and Fox society called the Midewiwin Society.

Sauk and Fox Emerging from Sweat House During Midewiwin Ceremony (ca. 1910)

Women rinse off members of the Midewiwin Society as they emerge from a sweat-lodge ritual held in the large, central tent.

Moccasin Game (ca. 1910)

A group of Shawnees play a shell game in which one player, using sleight of hand, hides an object under one of three moccasins and the other players try to guess which moccasin contains the object. The man hiding the object (wearing a blue shirt and a feather in his hair in this painting) must move it and the moccasins in time with a song he is singing; the other players smoke and keep time. The red and white folded blankets are probably the wager in the game.

continued from page 32

La Salle, the French officer and nobleman who founded St. Louis, described the Shawnees as "the best, finest, most intelligent and most skilled warriors in America."

In battle, the Shawnees were at their best on foot in a deep woods environment. In hand-to-hand combat, they were unequaled. The musket, the tomahawk, and the war club were the weapons they most preferred during warfare (bow and arrow were used primarily for hunting). Masters of stealth and ambush, powerful swimmers who were immune to even the iciest mountain streams and rivers, and tireless and remarkably skillful trackers, the Shawnees were an opponent their enemies would rather not encounter in the forests. Such was their expertise in woodland fighting and other woodland skills that the Shawnees acquired a supernatural *aura* as warriors and hunters. Other tribes believed that the Shawnees possessed powerful magic. The Shawnees were said to have the ability to transform themselves into animals and insects, to control the weather, and to become invisible at twilight. The Shawnees were indeed mysterious.

Frequently, a group of tribes would form an alliance to drive the Shawnees away from their territory. They were driven from the southeast by the Chickasaws and

Creeks, and from the Lake Michigan area by the Iroquois. In Pennsylvania, as well, they were continually harassed by the Iroquois. The Shawnees in Illinois were unhappy with the prairie environment of that region, so they also were soon on the move.

In 1725, one of the most powerful tribes in Middle America—the Miamis—offered the Shawnees a large section of their territory on the northern side of the *Spaylaywitheepi*— the Ohio River. The Miamis and Shawnees had been close allies since 1683, when the Ohio and Pennsylvania Shawnees, along with warriors of the Delaware peoples, had helped defend Miami territory against an Iroquois invasion. For the Miamis, this gift of land served to repay the debt they owed the Shawnees. The arrangement actually benefited both tribes: The Shawnees would finally have a permanent homeland. And the combination of the Shawnees and the Miamis, along with the Delawares and the ferocious Kickapoos situated nearby, would form an alliance that could stand up to any invaders— including, at that time, the Shemanese.

The widely scattered Shawnee bands began to converge on their new territory. Once separated, wandering east, west, north, and south, the Shawnees now came from all directions to the lands given to them by the Miamis. Perhaps they sensed the terrible crisis that loomed just over the horizon and knew that it was time to join together once again. Or perhaps they gathered together because they had finally found a homeland. Here, in the rich, fertile countryside along the north banks of the Ohio River, with its forests and fields and gently rolling hills; its diverse and abundant wildlife; its streams, lakes, ponds, waterfalls, and smaller branches of the great Spaylaywitheepi, the Shawnee nation was reborn.

CHAPTER 3

The Tomahawk and the Pipe

In the years following the Miamis' gift of territory to the Shawnees, Shawnee culture blossomed. Shawnees from all parts of North America ceased their wandering and traveled to the villages and towns that were springing up around the Ohio and Scioto rivers, as well as the Muskingum River, the Little Miami and Big Miami rivers, and the Mad River. By the 1740s, the Shawnees rivaled the Miamis as the most populous and powerful tribe in Middle America.

These were good years for the Shawnees. Day-to-day life in a Shawnee village was obviously appealing, judging by the number of white people who chose to become

A Shawnee hunter prepares to kill a deer. The woods in the Shawnees' territory were rich in game and other sources of food.

45

Shawnees after being captured. The Shawnees enjoyed life, and they lived well in the Ohio Valley. No better land for both hunting and farming could be found in America.

Corn was the Shawnees' principal food, but the Ohio Valley and the Kentucky woodlands were also teeming with wildlife—every kind of fowl imaginable, deer, otter, beaver, raccoon, rabbit, bear, turtles (for the delicious Shawnee turtle soup), birds of prey, and even forest buffalo. One-hundred-pound catfish were frequently hauled from the Ohio River and its tributaries.

Shawnee women gathered, grew, and prepared food for the tribe. Here, women collect tree sap and boil it down to produce sugar.

With this plentiful variety of food sources, Shawnee women became the most renowned of all Native American cooks. They were and still are especially famous for their cornbreads and fried corncakes. Members of tribes that were on friendly terms with the Shawnees—especially the Wyandots, Kickapoos, and Delawares—as well as white traders and travelers, always looked forward to visiting a Shawnee settlement simply for the food they were sure to be served.

The Shawnees enjoyed games, gambling, team sports, dancing, singing and chanting, and elaborate practical jokes. They also valued the simple pleasures of sitting with friends and relatives, talking, eating, and smoking, sometimes throughout an entire night if a long-absent friend or relative had arrived. Work was equally shared between men and women. A Shawnee male might help the women collect berries or prepare a dinner, while a female might ride off on the hunt or on the warpath.

Children were treated as gifts to be cherished. They were seldom, if ever, disciplined by hitting or spanking. The ultimate form of punishment was to embarrass and shame the child by talking about his or her misbehavior in front of other people. Good conduct was rewarded by praising the child's behavior in front of other members of the tribe, giving the child a sense of pride and self-respect. In this way, children were taught not only right and wrong but also that their behavior was important to the entire community.

The elderly were treated with great honor and respect. They formed special relationships with the children, sharing their knowledge and wisdom with the youngest members of the tribe.

Honesty was the single most important quality among the Shawnees. In discussion, council, or argument, everyone was expected to speak truthfully, no matter how harsh that truth might be. Lying was considered a crime. Except in matters of war, the Shawnees displayed generosity and love toward their neighbors. The golden rule of the Shawnee god Moneto was: "Do not kill or injure your neighbor, for it is not him that you injure, you injure yourself. But do good to him, therefore adding to his days of happiness as you add to your own."

Like all of the original peoples of North America, the Shawnees' cycle of activities was seasonal. During the summer, planting, hunting, and fishing provided food. In the fall were the harvest and a great tribal hunt to secure enough food for the winter. Ritual ceremonies honoring various spirits and gods surrounded seasonal events. The most important of these were the spring and fall Bread Dances and the midsummer Green Corn Dance. Through these ceremonies, the gods were given thanks for providing the Shawnees with food and life.

During the harsh, snow- and sleet-whipped winter of the Ohio River valley, a particularly dedicated young man—usually in his early teens or even younger—might engage in a quest for an *unsoma*. This process involved rising every morning at dawn, running naked through the snowy forest to a certain lake or pond, cracking the ice if there was any, diving to the bottom of the frigid waters, and then returning to camp. Under the instruction of an older warrior or a *shaman*, the process continued every morning for months. For his final dive, the young man was told to grasp whatever his hand first touched when he reached the bottom of the water and to retrieve it. Usually this was a stone or a pebble. This object would be the young man's unsoma—a power object to be worn on a string around the neck or carried in the young man's sacred bundle. (Sacred bundles were collections of spiritually related and magical objects carried in a leather pouch.) The unsoma brought its owner courage and luck in battle, as well as spiritual strength and wisdom.

And the grueling process involved in obtaining an unsoma built discipline, inner strength, and the ability to withstand extreme physical discomfort.

For the most part, however, the Shawnees remained inside during the winter, which was the most relaxed time of year. Extra bearskins and deerskins were hung from the walls and placed on the floors of the wegiwas, and people gathered around the fire. There was little need to venture outside, and the men rarely journeyed away to hunt or go on the warpath, so family groups were able to spend much time together. For children, winter was a time to learn about the Shawnee religion and to hear tales of heroes, spirits, and gods, and spooky stories of supernatural monsters, the magic of witches, and strange creatures of the deep forests.

The Shawnees had many such traditions and stories, and their religion was filled with numerous beings, both good and bad. Before missionaries brought Christianity to the tribes, the Shawnees had no concept of total evil. There was no figure similar to the devil in their religion. Some characters from their myths and spiritual beliefs were good and kind, and others were dangerous or mischievous. But none

A Native American woman carries her baby on her back while gathering firewood.

were utterly evil and determined to destroy or corrupt the Shawnees.

During the long winter nights, with the winds howling around the wegiwas, a Shawnee family would sit or lie about the fire, wrapped in animal robes and listening to one of the elders of the family tell a story of a great Shawnee battle or warrior or of some god or spirit. Many tales explained natural phenomena. Stars, for example, were the souls of deceased babies. The wind blowing through the trees at night might be the disembodied, shrieking head of some long-dead warrior cursed during his life by a witch and now flying through the forest at night. The coyote howling at midnight could be a shape-shifting witch casting a spell over some unlucky person. At times the Thunderbirds flew overhead, their great wings bringing storms, lightning, rain, and thunder.

Tornadoes were known as Cyclone Person. Cyclone Person was once a Shawnee woman of great spiritual power who began spinning around and around in order to capture the force of the Four Winds in her long hair. She became the swirling tornado, capable of uprooting trees and carrying away houses. But the Shawnees had no fear of Cyclone Person, who told them to build fires in their doorways when she appeared so that she could recognize them as Shawnees and pass over them without doing any harm. To this day, Shawnees have no fear when a tornado appears. They do not build storm cellars like the other people in Oklahoma, where they now live and where tornadoes are common. When a tornado comes, some of them sit on chairs on their porches and watch. Of course, they first build a fire in the doorway. Their homes are seldom, if ever, damaged by tornadoes.

The tales of Corn Woman and Pumpkin Woman and how they brought their gifts to the Shawnees were also related by the elders. Children were told about the Tree Men in order to teach them never to harm trees; the Shawnees believed that each tree was a living creature with its own inner spirit. The terrible Giant Horned Snakes, who lived underwater or in tunnels underground, and the frightening Flying Horse-Headed Snakes were spoken of in hushed tones. The two supreme beings, Moneto and Our Grandmother in the Sky, were spoken of with reverence.

The children were also told of the very foundation of the Shawnee religion—the five tribal sacred bundles. Each of the five divisions kept and protected one of the sacred bundles, which were older than

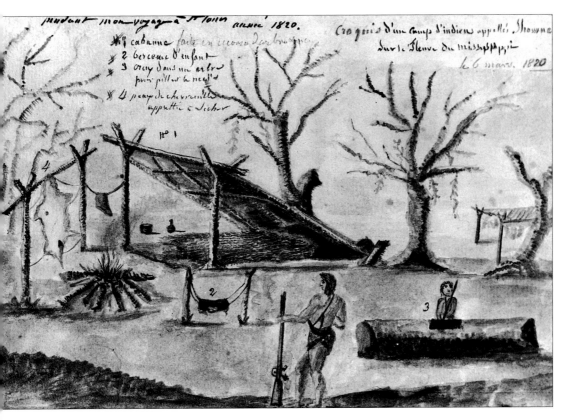

This painting from 1820 shows a Shawnee temporary camp. The numbered items are (1) a shelter made of poles and bark, (2) an infant's hammock, (3) a woman grinding corn in a hollowed log, and (4) a deerskin stretched for drying.

Shawnee history itself. Two of these bundles have survived to the present day. Their contents are unknown and have been unknown for centuries. One is believed to contain a scale from a Giant Horned Snake. The five sacred bundles represented the essence of Shawnee spirituality, and their contents were thought to represent the Shawnees' connection to the natural world, the spirit world, and the universe, all of which were, for the Shawnees, parts of a single interrelated whole.

In the spring, the snow melted and the cycle of life began again. The spring Bread Dance was celebrated, and planting began. Newlyweds often had their first child in the spring. The warriors rode off to travel and find battle.

The warriors often returned from battle with enemy captives. Not all those who were captured by the Shawnees were lucky enough to be adopted, like Blue Jacket. Adult warriors, soldiers, settlers, and scouts might instead be enslaved, although some were given food and a horse and sent on their way. Many unlucky prisoners were subjected to the most horrible of tortures and then executed, usually by being burned at the stake. This became more common in later years, when warfare between the whites and the Shawnees became extremely bloody and bitter.

The Shawnees have been described as both warlike and friendly; brutal and generous; vengeful and forgiving. Perhaps the tomahawk pipe best symbolizes the Shawnees. One side was a pipe used during religious ceremonies, peace councils, friendly encounters, or simple relaxation among friends and relatives. The other side of the same object was a hatchet used to split an enemy's head. Generally, the Shawnees would fight alongside or against any tribe, depending on the circumstances, and yesterday's enemies were often today's allies. Similarly, when Europeans began fighting each other in the Ohio Valley, the Shawnees joined the side that would most help them. In 1754, when fighting erupted between the French and the British over control of North America, many Shawnees sided with the French, who were more interested in trading with the Indians than in taking over their land. During the American Revolution, the Shawnees fought on the British side in hopes of halting the flow of American settlers into Shawnee territory.

Sometimes Shawnees found themselves opposing one another as allies of two warring powers. If this occurred, the Shawnees made sure to avoid killing one another in battle. Shawnee warriors liked to fight, and they were good at it. Simply put, the Shawnees were good to have as friends and bad to have as enemies. And by the middle of the 18th century, Shawnee warriors did not have to go far to find enemies. Despite their position of strength, their enemies were coming to them.

CHAPTER 4

The Panther

On the night of March 9, 1768, a huge comet appeared over the northern horizon. The comet traced a greenish-white streak across the heavens before disappearing in the southeast. People from Montreal to Memphis witnessed the spectacular event. Just as the comet's fiery tail vanished, the cry of a newborn baby was heard from a small tent pitched along Paint Creek, near the Scioto River in the Ohio River valley.

Sitting on logs near the iced-over creek, the baby's father, Pucksinwah—the renowned principal war chief of the Shawnee nation—and his teenage son, Chiksika, looked up in awe at the comet. As it disappeared, they

According to people who knew Tecumseh, this portrait, drawn by a French trader, is the most accurate likeness of him ever created.

57

heard the baby's cry, and the father knew that his wife, the Cherokee Methotasa, had given birth to a son. None of the midwives had to inform the principal war chief that the baby was a boy. Pucksinwah knew.

Pucksinwah knew many things before they happened. His family was gifted with the ability to foretell future events. Pucksinwah would accurately predict his own death and the circumstances surrounding it, as would his son Chiksika when his own time came. Pucksinwah also knew that his newborn son would be special—the passing of the comet at the moment of his birth was a clear sign.

Pucksinwah had doubts about bringing another child into the world at a time of war and terrible bloodshed, when the existence of the Shawnee tribe was in grave danger. For war now swirled about the Shawnees like a huge cyclone; a cyclone, Pucksinwah knew, that would not pass by the Shawnees like Cyclone Person.

Pucksinwah decided that the child must have a name reflecting the events of his birth. For the Shawnees, naming a child was an important act. Words possessed powerful magic, and a name was the most powerful of all words. The Shawnees believed that the name given to a newborn child played a large part in determining the child's character as well as the path the child's life would follow in the future. Shawnees who seemed to be leading unlucky or tragedy-filled lives often changed their names in an attempt to improve their fortune.

Usually, parents waited 10 days before naming a child. During this period they consulted with shamans—men and women with spiritual insight and power—and took part in various naming rituals and ceremonies. Often they waited until a shaman dreamed of a symbol that indicated what name the child should be given.

But Pucksinwah did not have to wait. This child's name was obvious. Shawnee legend tells of a great comet that was the spirit of a supernatural panther; a panther that periodically became visible as it circled the earth, searching for a resting place for the night. The Shawnee word for "Panther passing across"—the comet seen in flight—was *Tecumseh.* So the baby was named Tecumseh. And his passage across North American history would indeed be as spectacular and far reaching as the great comet that illuminated the skies on the night of his birth.

From the moment Tecumseh joined his first war party against the invaders—at the age of nine—he dedicated himself to de-

Native Americans and British commanders hold a council following Pontiac's War. Tecumseh's father, Pucksinwah, was a leader in the war, during which Indians of several tribes joined to fight the British.

fending the Native Americans' way of life. The fate of the Shawnees, and the fate of *all* the tribes of North America, would rest on his shoulders. Until Abraham Lincoln arrived to play his role in American history, there was no figure as great, and in the end as tragic, as Tecumseh. The tragedy of Tecumseh was that many Indians never realized that he was the one man who could hold off the flood of white expansion and the loss of Indian lands, Indian lives, and Indian culture. Had Abraham Lincoln never appeared, the United States would be a very different place today—a far worse place. And had all the tribes followed Tecumseh's vision, the United States might be a very different place as well. No doubt it would be a better place.

TECUMSEH.

CHAPTER 5

The Panther Crosses

Tecumseh's dignified manner, eloquent speech, and intelligence earned the admiration of all who met him, even his white enemies.

Exactly when Tecumseh's great vision crystallized in his own mind is hard to say. His grand plan seems to have formed bit by bit as he grew older. Tecumseh spent most of his teenage years traveling about the country with Chiksika. During his travels, he collected a small, intensely loyal band of followers from several different tribes. He fought alongside the Cherokee nation in its war against the whites. Back at home, along with Chiksika and Blue Jacket, he waged war against the whites who were flooding into Shawnee territory. By the age of 20, Tecumseh was known across Middle America; he had established a reputation among both whites and Indians as the most fearsome and intelligent warrior in the land.

Tecumseh preferred to fight on foot, using a war club. Although he was not a large man, he was quick, agile, and strong—indeed he was pantherlike—and he could not be beaten in hand-to-hand combat. As a leader, his sense of *strategy* remained un-equaled in Indian warfare until the appear-ance of the Lakota Sioux chief Crazy Horse. In battle, Tecumseh always did what his adversary least expected. In meetings with white leaders, he could be diplomatic, friendly, sarcastic, or downright intimidating, depending upon the circumstances.

Tecumseh's intelligence, even as a youth, was startling. He observed everything and asked countless questions, and his mind soaked up information like a sponge. He learned English and French and the lan-guages of many tribes.

Tecumseh's elders had no answer to many of the questions he asked. Although they were the most logical of questions, they were disturbing. Tecumseh's questions forced people to think about ideas they had always dismissed or had never questioned before. As he grew older, he developed a natural authority that even established war-riors and chiefs respected. At the age of 15,

The Shawnees sometimes tortured prisoners, tying them to a stake surrounded by a ring of fire. Tecumseh argued that torturing a helpless prisoner was the work of cowards.

the true depth of Tecumseh's wisdom and the strength of his personality became apparent.

Tecumseh was always disgusted and horrified by the Shawnee practice of torturing captives. One day, after a white captive was tortured and then burned alive, the 15-year-old Tecumseh told the warriors involved—including his older brother, Chiksika, and Blue Jacket, already a close friend—that he would never again speak to them or even recognize their existence if they continued to torture prisoners. A heated argument followed. Who was Tecumseh, at the age of 15, to challenge these highly respected warriors concerning a tradition that had been practiced centuries before he was even born? But the logic and the humanity of Tecumseh's argument, and the force of his personality, won out. No more torture would occur among Tecumseh's division (the Kishpokos)—at least not in his presence.

The single most important question Tecumseh asked was "Why do the Indians continue to fight each other when it is obvious that our true enemy is the white man?" Tecumseh realized that in fighting each other, the tribes were doing exactly what the whites wanted them to do—weakening each other and making it easier for whites to take over their land. Who were the most powerful peoples in America? The Iroquois and, by the turn of the century, the Americans. Why were they the most powerful? Two words answered this question for Tecumseh—*confederacy* and *united*, as in the Iroquois Confederacy and the United States.

During the running series of wars between the French and the English for control of North America, the Shawnees had fought, at one time or another, on both sides. The Shawnees had played a principal role in some of the most crushing defeats suffered by the British and the first American forces. But they had not fought alone; an alliance of tribes and whites had always been involved. As the 18th century came to a close, it was obvious that the greatest threat to the Shawnees was the United States. And it was obvious to Tecumseh that no single tribe, and no small alliance of tribes, could ever turn back the huge forces that would soon be directed against the Indians of America as the United States expanded relentlessly westward. There was, Tecumseh knew, only one way to stand up to the Americans and save the Shawnees—and all Indians—from having their world destroyed. By 1800, Tecumseh had begun the massive task of turning his vision into reality. Tecumseh's vision was nothing less than a great alliance, both in war and in spirit, of *all* the tribes of North America.

For ten years, Tecumseh traveled about North America, bringing his message to hundreds of tribes. Had the American government known exactly what he was up to, Tecumseh would have been imprisoned, or perhaps executed. (Actually, capturing Tecumseh would have been difficult. Tecumseh had the ability to make himself virtually invisible while he strolled through the midst of thousands of white people. Putting on white men's clothing, he would walk about a white city in a leisurely fashion, reading American newspapers and observing his enemies.)

In the meantime, Tecumseh's younger brother Tenskwatawa was spreading Tecumseh's spiritual message throughout the land. Tecumseh envisioned a spiritual as well as a military alliance among the tribes of America. At the core of this spirituality was a return to the way Indians had lived before white men contaminated their culture with disease, alcohol, and *materialism*. Tecumseh's religion called for Indians to shun white people and their ways. The Indians had to become self-sufficient again.

As he spread Tecumseh's gospel, Tenskwatawa gained a reputation as a teacher and *prophet*. To many, he was simply known as the Prophet. In reality, he was little more than Tecumseh's mouthpiece, but Tecumseh allowed his brother's reputation to grow. It kept the attention of the U.S. government and its spies on Tenskwatawa, allowing Tecumseh to roam the land freely, visiting tribes and forming his alliance.

By 1811, Tecumseh's skill as an *orator*, the logic of his argument, and the sheer force of his personality had won the allegiance of over 50 tribes. This was a monumental achievement. Ancient tribal grudges were put aside, and even tribes that had been mortal enemies of the Shawnees, such as the Mohawks, joined the alliance. The strongest resistance came from the Shawnees themselves. Many of the Shawnee chiefs were jealous of Tecumseh's power. Because of this rivalry, Tecumseh had moved away from the Shawnees, taking with him many Shawnee followers. In 1808, Tecumseh and Tenskwatawa had built a settlement called Prophet's Town on the Tippecanoe River. Tecumseh no longer considered himself a Shawnee, and he declared that he would never again fight against an Indian of *any* tribe.

Indians from all over flocked to Prophet's Town. Others waited in their own territory for Tecumseh's signal to begin the largest Indian uprising in history. Fifty tribes and tens of thousands of warriors would rise up across the country and drive the Americans back over the Alleghenies and, if possible, into the Atlantic Ocean. Realistically, Tecumseh knew that even the huge force he had organized could not totally defeat the Americans. But it would allow the Indians to negotiate with the United States from a position of strength, which was all that the Americans seemed to understand.

But history was not on the side of the Indians. In early November 1811, a huge U. S. army marched toward Prophet's Town. Tecumseh was away, as were the majority of his followers, who had gone off for an autumn hunt. Foolishly, Tenskwatawa, who had come to believe in his own image as a prophet, attacked the American force with only 350 warriors. Tenskwatawa promised the warriors that as long as he beat a sacred drum during the battle, the white soldiers' bullets could not harm them. As Tenskwatawa stood on a cliff overlooking the battle, beating his drum, the Indian force was crushed, and Prophet's Town was burned to the ground. Word of this disaster quickly spread, and Tecumseh's alliance began to crumble. Tecumseh returned to Prophet's Town to find ashes and the bodies of warriors. The survivors had scattered. Tenskwatawa was unharmed, but his reputation as a prophet and leader was ruined.

Despite the disaster of Prophet's Town, Tecumseh did not allow his dream to die. Loyal followers from many tribes returned to support Tecumseh, and soon he had a force of over 2,000 warriors under his command. In 1812, when war between the United States and England broke out, Tecumseh made a deal with the British. If he supported the British forces and they were victorious in defeating an American invasion into British-Canadian territory, Tecumseh and his followers would be granted the state of Michigan as a permanent homeland.

The Indian and British alliance scored a number of important victories, including the capture of Detroit, Chicago, and Fort Meigs in Ohio. But the Americans kept coming.

Tecumseh's brother Tenskwatawa lost an eye in a childhood accident. After seeing a vision of the Great Spirit, Tenskwatawa began preaching to the Indians and became known as the Prophet.

The final battle for Detroit and control of Lake Erie and the surrounding waterways was settled by the fleets of the Americans and the British. When the British fleet was wiped out, the British on the north side of the lake abandoned Detroit and went into retreat. Tecumseh begged, threatened, and cursed the British commander, who refused to make a stand against the Americans once their ships landed. Finally, the British general agreed to face the U.S. Army on the banks of the Thames River in Ontario, Canada. Tecumseh's troops, the British, and a force of Canadians—about 2,500 men altogether—would confront the oncoming Americans, who numbered around 4,000.

On the evening before the battle—October 4, 1813—Tecumseh summoned the inner core of his faithful allies to his tent. Gathered there were the Potawatomi chief Black Partridge; the Potawatomi Sauganash; the Wyandot chief Stiahta; Black Hawk of the Sacs; Carrymaunee of the Winnebagos; Waubansee, another Potawatomi; the Ojibwa brothers Ooshawanoo and Little Pine; Naiwash of the Ottawas; and Tecumseh's closest and most beloved friend, Chaubenee, another Potawatomi. As they sat in the flickering firelight, Tecumseh moved from man to man, touching each affectionately and giving each man one of his most prized personal possessions. He then informed them that he would be killed in the upcoming battle, and that the Americans would be victorious. His friends took his words seriously, for Tecumseh's gift as a prophet was well known and had been demonstrated many times. Horror and sorrow fell over the small group. Tecumseh then told his friends that any who wished to depart might do so, without dishonor. His friends elected to stay with him and die alongside him. Tecumseh then gave his final order—when he fell during the battle, his force must retreat and scatter, or they would all be destroyed.

During the battle, Tecumseh was shot twice through the heart and killed. For a few moments his warriors stood around his fallen body, furiously firing into the oncoming American troops. Then, remembering their leader's final command, they fled and scattered, disappearing like ghosts into the surrounding forest.

After the U.S. victory in the War of 1812, the Shawnees once again broke up into different bands and wandered. Some of them traveled to Missouri and joined the three breakaway divisions. A portion of that band broke off and traveled to Texas and settled among the

Cherokees. Some Shawnees traveled to Mexico, where a band of their old allies, the Kickapoos, were living. Unfortunately, most of them were stricken with bubonic plague and the band was almost entirely wiped out. Eventually, all of the Shawnees settled on three reservations in Oklahoma, where they remain to this day. The three groups are

During the Battle of Tippecanoe, 40 of Tecumseh's followers were killed and Prophet's Town was burned down.

known as the Absentee Shawnees, the Eastern Shawnees, and the Loyal, or Cherokee, Shawnees. The groups maintain close relations, but they have never reunited.

Unlike many other tribes, the Shawnees adapted well to reservation life. Their history of migration and their experience living among other tribes allowed them to make the most of their situation. They were, and still are, a strong and resilient people, always able to adjust to the requirements of their environment. Those aspects of white culture that they found favorable, they accepted. But they did not give up their traditional ways. Instead, they have managed to combine the two cultures in a way that best suits them. Many continued the Shawnee warrior tradition, enlisting in the U.S. Army and fighting in the Civil War and in American wars overseas, including World War II and Vietnam. Today, the Shawnees are among the most successful and prosperous of tribes. They work as ranchers and farmers, run businesses, live in modern houses and trailers, and drive cars. They also ride horses and practice the Green Corn Dance and many other traditional ceremonies. Two of the sacred tribal bundles remain among them. And in virtually every Shawnee home, a picture of Tecumseh hangs on the wall.

GLOSSARY

adapt   learn to live in a new environment

aura   a magical quality

culture   the language, traditions, and history of a people

exodus   a departure of a large group of people, usually to escape a bad situation

materialism   concern with obtaining objects that are not necessary for survival

oral history   history that is passed down through generations by word of mouth

orator   a person who delivers public speeches

prophet   a person who has the ability to foretell the future

shaman   a man or woman who has spiritual insight and power

strategy   a plan that is devised for a specific purpose

CHRONOLOGY

16th century The Shawnees settle in the lower Great Lakes region; after numerous attacks by the Iroquois Confederacy, the Shawnees break into small groups and scatter

1683 A band of Shawnees help the Miami Indians fend off an Iroquois invasion

1725 The Miamis grant the Shawnees a large section of territory north of the Ohio River; the Shawnees reunite in their new homeland

1754–63 During the French and Indian War, many Shawnees join the French in fighting the British

1768 Tecumseh is born

1775–83 The Shawnees fight on the British side during the American Revolution

1779 The Shawnee nation divides; three of the five Shawnee divisions depart from the Shawnees' war-torn homeland

ca. 1800 Tecumseh begins uniting Indians of all tribes in defending their lands

1804 Tenskwatawa begins spiritual movement that encourages Indians to unite and to abandon the ways of whites

1808 Prophet's Town is built; Indians from many tribes gather there to support Tecumseh

1811 U.S. Army destroys Prophet's Town during the Battle of Tippecanoe

1812 Tecumseh and his followers join the British in the War of 1812

1813 Tecumseh is killed at the Battle of the Thames

1814 After the U.S. victory in the War of 1812, the Shawnees scatter, eventually settling on three reservations in Oklahoma

INDEX